A Note to Parents

DK READERS is a compelling program for beginning readers, designed in conjunction with leading literacy experts, including Dr. Linda Gambrell, Director of the Eugene T. Moore School of Education at Clemson University. Dr. Gambrell has served on the Board of Directors of the International Reading Association and as President of the National Reading Conference.

Beautiful illustrations and superb full-color photographs combine with engaging, easy-to-read stories to offer a fresh approach to each subject in the series. Each DK READER is guaranteed to capture a child's interest while developing his or her reading skills, general knowledge, and love of reading.

The five levels of DK READERS are aimed at different reading abilities, enabling you to choose the books that are exactly right for your child:

Pre-level 1: Learning to read
Level 1: Beginning to read
Level 2: Beginning to read alone
Level 3: Reading alone
Level 4: Proficient readers

The "normal" age at which a child begins to read can be anywhere from three to eight years old, so these levels are only a general guideline.

No matter which level you select, you can be sure that you are helping your child learn to read, then read to learn!

LONDON, NEW YORK, MUNICH,
MELBOURNE, AND DELHI

Produced by Southern Lights
Custom Publishing

For DK
Publisher Andrew Berkhut
Executive Editor Mary Atkinson
Art Director Tina Vaughan
Photographer Keith Harrelson

Reading Consultant
Linda Gambrell, Ph.D.

First American Edition, 2001
04 05 06 10 9 8 7 6 5 4 3
Published in the United States by DK Publishing, Inc.
375 Hudson Street, New York, New York 10014

Published in Great Britain by Dorling Kindersley Limited

Library of Congress Cataloging-in-Publication Data
Hayward, Linda.
A day in the life of a reporter / written by Linda Hayward. --
1st American ed.
p. cm.
ISBN 0-7894-7956-7 -- ISBN 0-7894-7957-5 (pbk.)
1. Television broadcasting of news--Juvenile literature.
2. Reporters and reporting—Juvenile literature I. Title.

PN4784.T4 H39 2001
070.1'95--dc21   2001017392

Color reproduction by Colourscan, Singapore
Printed and bound in China by L. Rex Printing Co., Ltd.

The characters and events in this story are fictional and do not represent real persons or events.

The publisher would like to thank the following for their kind permission to reproduce their
photographs:
Key: t=top, b=bottom, l=left, r=right, c=center
DK Picture Library: Dave King front cover. Models: Stephanie Aaron, Mac Bethea, Anna
Cowan, Kapil Desai, Steve Gates, Gonzalo Gurmendi, Natalia Gurmendi, Andrea Hand,
Christopher Holby, Tim Jones, Duke LaGrone, Thomas Lower, Ben Philpott, Cassandra Porter,
Mira Rubin, Haley Spratt, and Marliese Thomas.

In addition, Dorling Kindersley would like to thank Shirley Harden and ABC 33/40,
Birmingham, Alabama for location photography, and Joe Miele of Diamond Studios for props.

All other images © Dorling Kindesley Limited
For further information see: www.dkimages.com

Discover more at
www.dk.com

DK READERS

A Day in the Life of a TV Reporter

Written by Linda Hayward

DK Publishing, Inc.

Mark Garcia listens to the radio
as he gets ready for work.
He needs to know the news.
Mark is a TV reporter.

Mark's daughter, Sara,
gets ready for school.

Mark takes Sara to school.
Then he goes to the TV station.

At the TV station, Mark sees Jen.
She works the camera.

camera

"Are you ready
for the news-team meeting?"
asks Jen.
"Yes," says Mark.

The team decides what stories to report for tonight's news. Mark says that a local school is cleaning up a river.

Laurie is the producer.
She is in charge of the news.
"Mark and Jen can report
on the clean up," says Laurie.

videotape

Mark finds
an old videotape.
It shows how clean
the river used to be.

He writes some notes
about the videotape
in his notebook.
He can use them
in his report.

notebook

Mark and Jen drive to the river.
Lots of people are there.
Mark starts talking
to the students.
Jen starts videotaping.

Mark's cell phone rings.
"How's the clean up going?"
asks Laurie, the producer.
"It's going well," says Mark.
"It will be a good story."

cell
phone

Mark sees Ellen and Steve
from the local newspaper.
They are interviewing
one of the students.

Ben is a reporter
from a radio station.
He is recording the story
on a tape recorder.

tape
recorder

Jen points the camera at Mark. "People used to swim in this river, but now it is full of trash," says Mark.

Jen points the camera
at the students.
"Today these students
are cleaning up the river,"
Mark says.

Page and Libby
are picking up cans.
Page sometimes baby-sits Sara,
Mark's daughter.
She sees Mark and waves to him.

Mark holds
the microphone
up to Page.

microphone

"What do you want to see?"
he asks.
"A clean river!" cries Page.

Suddenly there is a shout.
"Look what I found!" calls Libby.
She holds up a metal box.
It has jewelry and money inside!

Jen takes a shot of Libby
with the box.
"We'll put this on the news,"
says Mark.
"Maybe we'll find the owner!"

Mark and Jen are excited.
"This is a big story now,"
says Jen.

They pack up the camera
and go back to the TV station.

Brian, the technician, edits
the tape on the TV screen.
Mark tells Brian
which parts to use.

TV screen

Now the story is ready
for the news.
Mark leaves to pick up Sara
from school.

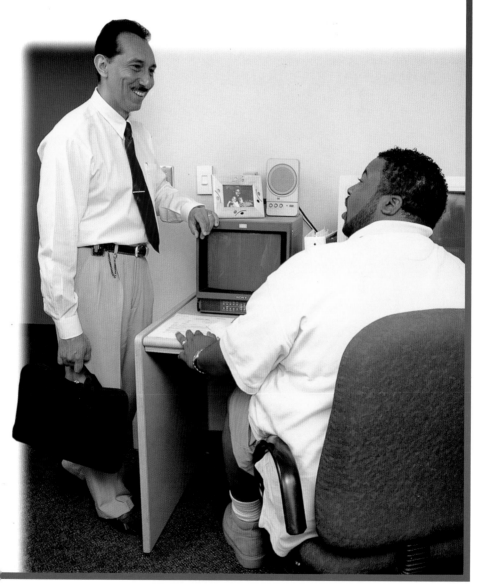

At home, Sara and Mark
talk about the day.
"Did you see Page?" asks Sara.
"Yes," says Mark.
"Her friend found
a box of treasure!"

Back at the TV station,
the cameras and studio lights
are on.

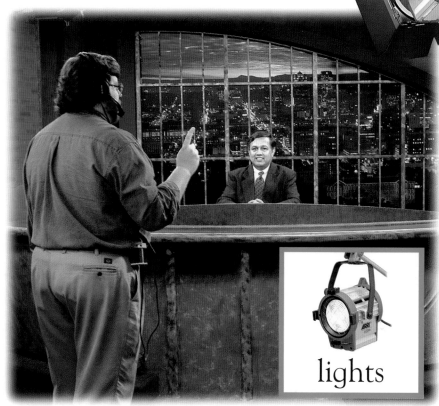

lights

Max, the director, makes sure
everything happens on time.
He tells Bob to start reading
the news.

"There was an exciting find at the river clean up today," says Bob.

After the news,
Mark's phone rings.
It is Laurie, the producer.

"The box of jewelry and money was stolen property," says Laurie. "The lady who owns it called the station. She's giving the money to the river clean up!"

"Dad, you did a great job!"
says Sara.
"I can't wait to tell
everyone at school!"

Mark smiles.
He has the best job in the world.

Picture Word List

camera page 7

tape recorder page 15

videotape page 10

microphone page 19

notebook page 11

TV screen page 24

cell phone page 13

lights page 27